STICKY CUSTOMER SERVICE

Stop Churning Customers and Start Growing Your Business

-

PETER LYLE DEHAAN

Sticky Customer Service: Stop Churning Customers and Start Growing Your Business © 2021 by Peter Lyle DeHaan.

Book 1 in the Sticky series.

ISBN
  978-1-948082-58-7 e-book
  978-1-948082-59-4 paperback
  978-1-948082-60-0 hardcover

Published by Rock Rooster Books

Credits:
  Developmental editor: Kathryn Wilmotte
  Copy editor/proofreader: Robyn Mulder
  Cover design: Taryn Nergaard
  Author photo: Jordan Leigh Photography

To all who serve others.

Contents

Customer Service Matters

We hear much today about delighting our customers. This is an admirable goal, and every business should strive to do so. We must acknowledge, however, that this is not sustainable. We may delight customers upon occasion, but to expect we'll succeed in every interaction will leave us falling short of their increasingly higher standards.

Each time we do something that excites our customers, we set the bar higher for next time. What delights them today and gets them to tell their friends about us will soon fade into the recesses of normalcy. Then, when we can't meet their newly heightened expectations, we have much further to fall and their disappointment will be all that much greater.

Instead, we should set a more realistic goal. Though it's not exciting or compelling, we should aim simply to meet customer expectations. Though this sounds boring, don't dismiss the idea too fast. Many customer service interactions fall short—sometimes far short—of meeting customers' expectations.

Meeting expectations is sustainable and is good business.

Do you know someone who left one company because of service issues and then left the new company for the same reason? Once they have used and dismissed each company, their new goal is to pick the least objectionable one.

They no longer pursue the best option. Instead, they seek the one that is least bad, returning to a former unsatisfactory provider. This produces a revolving door of customer churn, whereas a better goal is to keep existing customers.

Does any company provide quality service anymore? The good news is yes, and I celebrate this whenever possible. Yet for each positive example, it's usually not the company but one person who made the difference. They cared about me and had a genuine interest in the outcome. I was their priority, and they did what the situation required.

Every company claims they offer quality service, but is it real or fantasy? Is a personal connection provided to customers? Can you say, believe, and prove that your company delivers quality service? If you can't, what changes do you need to make?

* * *

Throughout my career, from the jobs I've held, businesses I've managed, and companies I've owned, a consistent thread has been customer service in one form or another. Yet I'm not writing about my experiences in providing customer service, for we are our own worst judges of success. And I'll admit to having fallen short too many times.

Though sharing a lifetime of experience in providing customer service would offer useful input, it would only draw from the businesses I've owned and managed. Instead, this book covers something I have much more experience with. Not in *providing,* but in *receiving* customer service—and in *not* receiving it.

We can glean a far better perspective by looking at a lifetime of receiving customer service. This provides a greater array of consideration, offering a more comprehensive approach that most customer service books miss.

I am a consumer. As someone who purchases products and services, I often need support after the sale. I need customer service. In this book, I'll share the times that left me appalled or produced discouragement. Yet I'll also share those times— albeit not as common—when I experienced customer satisfaction.

Customer service opportunities occur in three arenas. These are in person, over the telephone, and online. None functions in isolation. Each type of customer-focused communication informs our expectations in the other formats. Regardless of the communication channel, whether we're speaking face to face, talking on the phone, or interacting over the internet, we deal with the same issues and desire the same outcomes.

It's my hope that this book will provide you with helpful customer service insights that will encourage you to do better and celebrate what you do best. Let us meet our consumers' expectations every chance we get.

In-Person Customer Service

W̲e'll start our exploration with in-person interactions. These normally occur in retail, service, and hospitality settings.

Insights that we gain from these in-person customer service opportunities, however, can inform our perspectives regardless of how and where the customer connection takes place.

Is It Business or Personal?

Build Relationships to Forge
Ongoing Business

When I did a lot of printing, I used what was essentially the same printer for my business forms. I used them for years. Our time together bridged many changes. For me, it transcended two places of employment. For them, it spanned three ownerships, a time of expansion and contraction, three name changes, and a merger. We stayed together through it all—until they messed things up.

It Starts with Friendliness

This printer was near my office, had competitive prices, and was easy to work with. Convenience, price, and service were all significant reasons to use them. So begins my story.

What impressed me the most, however, was their collective friendliness. It didn't matter who I talked with. Whether on the phone or in person, they were always friendly. After friendliness is acquaintance, which leads to relationship. I knew the staff and the owner—who never felt it beneath him to wait on me. We had a relationship. With relationship comes understanding, tolerance, and forgiveness.

Although they exemplified the adage to "under promise and over deliver," at times things didn't go as expected. Sometimes this was my fault and other times theirs, but regardless we worked through these glitches for the common good of our long-term relationship. I understood they were in business to make money and that I needed to be a profitable account. Likewise, I needed quality product.

Form a Relationship

When a problem occurred, if we didn't have a rapport, instead of seeking our mutual benefit, we would have sought our individual self-interest. We would have pursued mutually exclusive goals and become adversarial.

Instead, we pursued a relationship. Relationship creates tolerance. Tolerance overlooks the small stuff, the issues that aren't essential. If they made a mistake that didn't affect the form's essential usefulness, my tolerance accepted the product.

However, if a problem occurred integral to its function, then reprinting was in order. Our relationship prompted their desire to correct errors, while tolerance gave me the desire to allow for extra time.

The last relational benefit is forgiveness. If they missed a deadline, I wanted to forgive them. If I had a rush job or changed something mid-production, they forgave my lack of planning.

One day, as I walked from their front door to the counter, three people paused their work, glanced up, and greeted me by name. They were glad to see me, and I was happy to be there. Bob approached me and beamed. "We're the printer where everybody knows your name!" He was right. They knew my name, making me feel welcomed and appreciated.

Bob and I got to know each other. Our kids were in marching band at their respective schools, giving us a commonality apart from business. Although not a hunter, I enjoyed hearing of his adventures in the woods. He heard of my business trips and home improvement projects. When Bob bought into the business, he shared his news with me. As business owners, we now had another area of connection.

I changed jobs and Bob's downtown shop was no longer convenient for me, but I kept going anyway. When he moved to manage a satellite store, I followed him there. It was also closer for me. Later, when a downturn in the economy required the closure of his location, my loyalty followed him to a third store. Though not as convenient, the extra drive was worth it to see my old friend.

Avoid Transactions

Then they merged with another company. This resulted in yet another name change and the closing of Bob's satellite office. Later, needing to have some envelopes printed, I returned to their original location. I hoped to find Bob there and the other people I'd known for so long. I saw nobody I knew, and no one knew me. They didn't understand my history that spanned decades. They weren't friendly and didn't try to know me. I represented an order, not a relationship. I was a transaction, not a friend.

It's not that these things are essential to printing envelopes, business cards, or flyers, but they are a pleasant bonus. A personal connection with my printer didn't improve the quality of the final product. In a hard-core business sense, these things don't matter. Or do they?

When I picked up my order, the bill shocked me. Their rates had gone up a lot. I hadn't checked. I gave the new regime the trust earned by the old one, paying for my lapse. Back at my office, opening the box of envelopes again distressed me. There were problems with two of the first twenty. A 10 percent error rate is not the quality I expected. The frequency of faulty product dropped as I worked through the box, but that initial impression stuck with me.

In the past, I would have called Bob and we would have worked something out, but now I didn't know who to contact. There was no relationship anymore, so there was no real reason to maintain it. My mind was already searching for another printer.

Conclusion

I learned we need to get personal with those we do business with. Relationships matter. Then, when results fall short of expectation, we can work together to develop a solution that benefits us both. If a minor problem occurs, tolerance will win out and forgiveness can take place. If the business moves, the name changes, or new owners show up, it's the personal relationships that hold customers close and keep them from seeking out the competition.

So get personal. It's good business.

Customer Service Success Tip

Move from a transaction mindset to a relationship perspective.

Customer Service
Is Not a Slogan

Lessons for All from the Auto Repair Industry

D oes your organization make customer service a priority? I expect it does. In fact, I suspect the phrase "customer service" occurs somewhere in your mission or vision statement and appears on a wall plaque, a statement that your marketing material hypes. In addition, upper management often talks about providing quality customer service.

However, as the saying goes, "talk is cheap." Another saying reminds us that "actions speak louder than words."

Do you deliver quality customer service or just talk about it? Have you said "world-class service" so often that you—and the entire organization—become convinced it's a reality, when in fact it isn't?

Customer Service Failure

An unacceptable experience at a car dealership was the incentive I needed to return to the trustworthy comfort of my local service station, where I continue to be a loyal customer of their car care services.

Yet the dreaded day came when they informed me that they weren't willing to tackle repairing my heat-producing air conditioner. I would need to take my car back to the *dealer*.

With trepidation, I entered the dealer's well-lit and decorated service department. As I walked up to the "customer service" desk, a representative, clad in business attire with a tasteful tie, greeted me by name—even though I'd not been there in a couple of years. I explained the problem and, knowing their mode of operation all too well, asked for an estimate. With a confidence-building smile and positive words of assurance, he agreed.

His phone call came soon after I returned to my office: $1,575. After my dumbfounded silence, he launched into an extended explanation, mixing mechanic jargon and automotive terminology, which I doubt even he understood. His aim, I assume, was to intimidate me into accepting their costly diagnosis. Their investigation also uncovered a heater problem that somehow related to the AC repair. True, for only $980, I could fix just the AC, but then it would be over $1,200 to go back *later* to repair the heater.

"Let's get realistic." I challenged him, determined not to be a victim of their predatory practices once again.

The representative apologized, saying he had no other options. "My hands are tied."

I declined to approve the repair and later picked up the car.

"I'm sorry," he kept repeating. "I know I've lost you as a customer."

He was right.

Customer Service Success

After some time, I finally found a full-service garage with a reputation for honesty. I took the car in. Sitting in a small and dingy office, with dated décor and amid organized clutter, I explained the chronology of events, sharing the dealer's written estimate.

The owner of the garage chose his words with care. "Well, they could be right, but I think we can get it working for much less." He had a $185 solution that he wanted to try. Plus, if his diagnosis proved wrong, he would apply that amount to the repair the dealer recommended, for which his price was only $800. As far as the heater issue, he found no justification for any repairs.

I followed his recommendation. The $185 AC repair worked, keeping us cool through a sizzling summer. The heater performed without incident throughout that winter, and for many years after, for as long as we owned the car.

The dealership talked ad nauseam about their top-notch customer service in their ads, promotions, mailings, and sales pitch. They put on an impressive front but provided little substance. To them, their customer service goal seemed to be to maximize the repair bill.

The garage, however, didn't talk customer service; they just did it.

Customer Service Success Tip

Uncover and fix practices in your business that are a disservice to your customers and drive them away.

Customer Service Is a Strategy

Lessons for All from Retail

Renting movies from a video store is not as common as it once was. Yet the lessons from this long-ago story aren't about movie rental stores, not really. Instead, it's a commentary on every retail business and just as applicable to online commerce.

How to Lose at Customer Service

Although my family is not prone to rent movies, we did have a membership at an outlet in a nearby town. My wife and I entered the store, with a two-for-one coupon in hand and the residual amount from a gift certificate on account. Our expectation was that we would each pick a movie and pay for them using the coupon and credit balance.

We were wrong.

The first sign of trouble came in the checkout line, when the clerk couldn't find our account in the computer. "We got new computers." He continued pounding the keyboard in vain. "When were you last here?"

Our answer irritated him.

"Well, that's your problem," he announced. "We gotta put ya back in." He took all our information and had us sign an ominous contract.

As he scanned the DVDs, I handed him the coupon.

"We don't accept these."

"Why?"

"It's for Acme Video Hits and we're Acme Video Plus."

I pointed to the in-store sign displaying Acme Video Hits. "We got bought out, and they voided all the coupons. We haven't changed our signs yet." He typed some more. "That will be seven dollars."

"You charged us the price for current releases." I pointed to a sign for 99 cent rentals of older movies.

"They changed that too." An unfruitful discussion ensued. He left to get the manager when I inquired about our credit balance, which had disappeared during either the acquisition or the computer upgrade.

The manager arrived. He summarized the information we had pieced together from the uncaring clerk. Next, he stated the company line and confirmed the price of seven dollars. When I objected, he relented and offered to accept our coupon in part, zero out the balance on our unverifiable account, and only charge us three dollars.

Sensing this was the best we could achieve, I accepted his offer.

He beamed and shook my hand, no doubt assuring himself of a resolved conflict and a kept customer.

My wife and I left with the opposite perspective. The careless clerk had dug too deep of a hole for his boss to climb out of. The damage he did was irreversible. We watched and returned the movies and never came back.

How to Win with Customer Service

It wasn't until another movie rental chain opened a local outlet that we again rented a movie. We walked in. With hesitation, I approached the counter. The manager smiled and welcomed us with genuine warmth. Upon learning we were first-time customers, she explained with much care how everything worked. This included the store layout, membership, prices, and specials. Her pleasant and easygoing demeanor was refreshing and put us at ease.

As we browsed, clerks would walk up. They'd restate a tidbit of information, provide direction, or offer their help. Then they'd move away as quickly as they appeared. This was not like my usual retail experience.

In most cases, when a clerk asks if I need help, I feel compelled to say no even if I do. At this movie rental store, the clerks' interactions were both welcomed and beneficial.

When it came time to pay, the manager, with her effervescent personality and obvious enjoyment of her job, made becoming a member both pleasant and easy. She restated the value of membership and reminded us of the specials. She even did a successful upsell—which seldom works with me—to prepay for several movies.

This was quite a feat considering my prior experience with having an unusable credit balance. But when someone offers a compelling deal, presented with infectious enthusiasm, it's easy to say yes.

The manager amazed me even further because during all this she was training two employees. She gave them subtle cues and brief instructions while serving us, without leaving us feeling slighted or inconvenienced.

It's not surprising that I looked forward to my next movie rental. I even planned my selections for that snowy weekend when I would take advantage of their "buy two, get three free" special.

Memorable customer service is always an invitation to return.

Customer Service Success Tip

Successful customer service starts and ends with frontline staff. Make sure you have the right people in place. Train them thoroughly and empower them to do what's needed to best serve customers.

Get Mad to Get Results

Don't Train Customers to Yell

Once I traveled to a convention with a female associate. The registration desk at the hotel had long lines. At last, we advanced to the front, where we learned that only my room was available. They had canceled my coworker's reservation. The hotel was sold out.

"Can you share a room?"

"That's unacceptable." I repeated our confirmation numbers.

"Your confirmation was canceled."

"But I didn't cancel it." It was then that I realized a confirmation number meant nothing if a hotel intended to not give you a room.

At three in the afternoon not everyone had checked in, so there were rooms available. Though it was possible they had all the rooms booked, many were no doubt unoccupied at that moment. I knew with persistence we could get room number two.

First, I insisted they provide our second room. I was polite, yet firm.

Next, I tried an emotional plea, but the clerk remained unmoved. I was getting nowhere.

Escalate the Situation

I knew what I needed to do.

I gathered my resolve and voiced my request at a much louder volume, something most uncharacteristic of me. The area was full of other guests waiting in line, so I garnered a bit of attention with my louder demand that they give me the room they guaranteed. It wasn't long before the clerk excused herself and summoned the manager. He arrived right away.

With a broad smile, he greeted me by name and offered his hand. He seemed well-schooled in problem-resolution techniques—but so was I. Giving him an icy stare, I didn't budge. Once I had communicated my agitation, I extended my hand with hesitation, while maintaining my penetrating stare. My ploy was working, so it was hard not to smile.

"I understand there's been a misunderstanding about your reservation," he said with low-key calmness.

"There's been no misunderstanding. I want the room I reserved, and that you guaranteed." I still talked in a louder-than-normal voice.

He began applying his conflict resolution skills to calm me down. With proficiency, he maneuvered me away from the other guests. I agreed, to let him sense he was prevailing. He guided me to a chair and said he would see what he could do. He returned a few minutes later with the second room. For the first time, I permitted my smile to appear. I shook his hand and thanked him. The entire ordeal of checking in took thirty minutes.

If I persisted, I knew they would give us two rooms. So why didn't management authorize the desk clerk to assess the problem and solve it, without me having to act mad or her needing to summon the manager?

Too often businesses do this with their customer service employees. Managers make their staff endure the wrath of irate customers—who've learned to yell to get their way—without granting staff the authority to resolve the problem.

Just empower people to do the jobs you hired them to do. Everyone will benefit.

Customer Service Success Tip

Ask your customer-facing staff how you can better empower them to do their jobs and meet customer expectations.

An Eye for Customer Service

*Treat Customers Right to Keep Their Business
and Gain New Business*

I t was an emergency run to the eye doctor. Being farsighted and using a computer all day makes glasses indispensable—a tool I treat with the utmost care. Imagine my dismay when during my morning cleaning routine the frame snapped, and a lens landed in my hand. I was panic-stricken. How could I work?

I arrived at my optometrist's office just as the doors opened. I explained the situation and, though they treated my disaster as routine, I found comfort in their willingness to help.

"We'll need to order new frames," the man concluded.

"Can't you just fix them?" I begged.

"We could," he droned, "but there's no guarantee. It might hold a day, maybe a few months. Don't worry," he added, "we'll get you some loaner frames to use while you wait for your new ones."

Trusting his advice, I assented.

Questionable Guidance

He disappeared into a back room and returned several minutes later. The look on his face braced me for unwelcome news. "Your frames have been discontinued. We'll have to fix your old ones. We can solder them."

Over the years, I've done my share of soldering: in electronics to make an electrical connection and in plumbing to seal a joint. I knew solder would not repair my damaged frames for more than a few minutes. I voiced my apprehension.

He smiled and clarified. "It's more like welding."

Now I knew he was off base. During a stint working at a machine shop, I did more types of welding than most people know exist. I didn't see any of those methods working to repair my delicate wire-rims. But I was out of options, so I consented.

He outlined the details: they would send out my broken frames for repair. They'd be back in a few days—maybe Saturday. It would cost twenty dollars.

He then set out to find a loaner frame. After half an hour with no success, he at last uncovered one old demo pair that, although not the right dimensions, would at least hold my lenses in their approximate place. The temple pieces were too short, which tipped the lenses forward, throwing off the bifocals.

I could adapt. I must. Grateful for a solution, albeit uncomfortable and less than ideal, I reminded myself that it was only for a few days and thanked him.

His parting promise left no doubt as to what I should expect. "We'll call you when your frames come back—let's hope for Saturday."

A Broken Promise

As I left, I confirmed the plan at the front desk. "Yes," she affirmed, "we'll call when your frames come in."

I trusted her.

Saturday came without a call. They were closed on Monday. I phoned them on Tuesday. I got an answering machine. Dismayed that they did not answer their phone in the middle of the day, I left a message imploring them to call. No one did. On Wednesday, I called again.

"Sure, they're here. You can stop in anytime." She said this as though getting my glasses fixed and returning my life to normal was a trivial matter.

By now, the tops of my ears were inflamed, and the bridge of my nose was tender because of the ill-fitting frames. "I'll be there in twenty minutes."

Bad Records

The man greeted me soon after I arrived. "It will only take a few minutes to switch lenses," he said with a smile. I reminded him that the screws holding my lenses in my frames loosen and fall out.

"Don't worry," he assured me, "I'll put in special screws that are chemically treated."

"No," I said. "You've done that before, and they still fall out. Last time you said you 'glued them.'" Because of this problem, he had reinstalled my lenses four times in the past three years. Why wasn't this critical information in my file?

He said nothing, but gave a slight nod of comprehension, retreating into his work area. A few minutes later, he returned, and I donned my restored glasses. What a great feeling. It was just like slipping into a comfortable pair of old shoes.

An Epic Fail

I thanked him and segued to my next goal. "Will you please put my old lenses in another frame—any frame," I inquired, "so that I can have a backup pair?"

"Your frames have been discontinued," he said, telling me what I already knew.

"Someone must make a frame that will fit my lenses," I prodded.

"I already looked, remember?" Now he was getting irritated with me. "You'll need to order new frames and get new lenses, and before we'll do that, you'll need an eye exam."

"That will be almost five hundred dollars. I can only afford a second frame."

"You should have an eye exam every year," he lectured. "It's been fourteen months for you."

"I just want a backup frame," I pleaded.

His reply was curt. "Sorry. We can't help you." He turned and walked away.

An Alternate Solution

I mentioned my ordeal—and desire for a backup pair of glasses—to my mother. Mom took this as a personal challenge and the next day surprised me with a list of businesses willing to assist. Two days later, I visited the top one on her list. Their office was closer, easier to get to, and had free parking at the door.

I walked in, explained my plight to the receptionist, and shared my goal. I waited a few minutes and an empathetic young lady greeted me. She listened to my tale of woe, acknowledging that it, too, would have been their preference for an exam, new frames, and new lenses.

But she pledged to try her best to help. She began to search for suitable frames, and I realized her intent was to handle my request right then. She came back with a frame that she hoped would work with some adjustments or by grinding my lenses. I had not expected an immediate resolution, and since there were several other customers waiting, I told her I'd be more than happy to come back later. She thanked me and promised to work on my glasses first thing the next day. I could stop by anytime.

I trusted her.

The next afternoon I returned. She recognized me and approached, beaming. "I have your glasses done," she glowed with the pride of an artist. "I'm really pleased with how they turned out."

Based on her sincerity, I knew I'd be pleased as well. She only charged me for the frames. There was no labor fee. She gave me a free case and a discount too. With much appreciation, I thanked her. She said she was glad she could help.

On my first visit, I noticed a sign that gave their repair rates. To solder frames was only five dollars. My old optometrist had charged four times as much. Five dollars would not cover shipping, so I assumed they did the repairs in-house. I suspected I wouldn't have to wait eight days either.

I'd already decided they would be my new optometrist, but I took one more step to confirm my decision. "How much is an eye exam?" I asked. It was fifty dollars less than what I had been paying. I set up an appointment.

By giving poor customer service, my eye doctor had lost a long-time customer. By going the extra mile, someone else gained one.

How to Lose Business

- Act apathetic toward your customer's situation.

- Make promises you don't keep.

- Don't listen to your customers.

- Make self-serving recommendations.

- Fail to keep accurate records.

- Give customers a reason to check out your competition.

How to Gain Business

- Be genuine and sympathetic, even if it's a routine matter for you.

- Only make promises you can keep.

- Listen to what customers say.

- Gain credibility by going the extra mile.

- Make sure your customer's interaction with you is memorable.

- Give customers a reason to never return to their old provider.

My old optometrist closed a couple years later. Given my experience with them, I'm not surprised.

It's much easier to keep an existing customer than to gain a new one. Where do you place your emphasis?

Customer Service Success Tip

Treat your customers like gold—because they are even more valuable.

Customer Rip-Offs

Make Sure Your Objectives
Align with Your Practices

To avoid the huge depreciation loss that all new cars undergo, I buy used. However, there was a season when I bought new. This story is about one of those times.

Although it wasn't my practice to go to the dealer for maintenance, my new car changed that habit. There was warranty work and the enticement of coupons for low-cost oil changes.

Soon my default destination for auto service changed. It was smart marketing on their part. When the discounts stopped, I still returned to them for service. Too bad their later actions drove me away.

An Expensive Oil Change

It was time for my regular service, and I had a list of other things needing attention. Since I'm not a mechanic, I tried not to tell them what work to do. Instead, I informed them of symptoms. I wanted to make sure that I didn't ask and pay for a tune-up when the problem may have been a loose vacuum hose. It only took one passive-aggressive mechanic to do what I suggested—while ignoring the real problem—to make me change my approach.

When I dropped off my car, I said, "It's time for an oil change. Also, it pulls to the right, and it starts hard and runs rough." I left expecting they would change the oil, do a front-end alignment, and give my car a tune-up. Based on their posted pricing, I estimated the cost would be $100.

When I picked up my car, they presented me with a $175 bill. As I read the paperwork, my mild surprise changed to anger.

Change oil: Oil, lube, filter, labor: $24.95.

Car pulls to right: Test drove car; *recommend* front-end alignment: $19.95.

Hard to start: *Instruct* driver not to press gas pedal while starting vehicle: $56.00.

Runs rough: Perform engine analysis; checks okay; *do tune-up in 3,000 miles*: $75.00.

For $175, I had my oil changed and received some costly advice. My complaints to the service manager accomplished nothing, so I left and never returned. Once again, my local mechanic, whom I trust to do quality work and charge fair prices, is servicing my cars.

Like many businesses, car dealers measure the work their employees do. Garages monitor mechanics to make sure they're productive throughout the day, document and bill for all their work, and complete repairs within the standard time allotment. Mechanics who meet expectations receive raises and promotions. Mechanics who don't, even when it's in the customer's best interest, earn poor reviews and lower raises. Or they're fired.

Some garages pay their mechanics based on billable work. Therefore, the more they bill, the more they make. I've been to those places too. At one shop specializing in foreign car repair, it seemed every bill was always around $500—sometimes more. They weren't in business long.

Other people also bill by time. Lawyers and accountants come to mind. A lawyer once told me to never use an attorney trying to make partner. To get the partners' attention, they must log over 2,000 billable hours a year, and their clients pay the price.

A Costly Failure

I once called my CPA's office to discuss converting my IRA to a Roth IRA. I talked with the junior member they'd assigned to me, asking if there were any other tax ramifications I should know about. She said there weren't and offered to do an analysis for me.

"That's not necessary," I replied. "You confirmed what I needed."

"But we just got this new program that I want to try out," she begged. "Will you let me run an analysis?" Assuming I was doing her a favor, I consented. The call took less than a minute. A few days later, I received a one-page spreadsheet confirming I should switch to a Roth IRA, along with a bill for $100.

The managing partner agreed the charge was unwarranted, but insisted I pay it anyway. He promised to make it up to me later.

I found a different tax advisor.

An Inflated Bill

Though people don't have their TVs repaired anymore, this wasn't always the case. Long ago a friend landed a summer job repairing televisions. He earned 20 percent of whatever he billed. An enterprising guy, he analyzed the rate chart and determined how to add $35 to each bill—for which he'd earn $7—for only a minute and a half of additional work.

He would take the back off the unit and hit it with a burst of compressed air, charging $8.00 to "clean chassis." Next, he would squirt the tuner with cleaning spray, charging $10.50 to "lubricate tuner." Then he would turn on the set. If the filaments of the vacuum tubes glowed, he would bill $16.50 to "check all vacuum tubes." With $35 of basic tasks completed, he would then repair the problem, adding even more to the bill.

He earned a lot of money that summer.

Measuring Business Success

There's an old business saying (of disputed origin), that "What gets measured gets done." Some have tacked on a follow-up adage that "What gets paid for gets done better."

Consider what you measure in your business and how you compensate your staff. The goal is to improve your operation. This could be to pursue greater efficiency, increase production, decrease costs, or maximize revenue.

Consider the consequences with care.

Attempting to please you, maximize their rating, or earn a raise, employees may do things that drive away customers, lower quality, or hurt your business. This is the wrong outcome.

If you monitor productivity, do your staff members alter their work habits to *appear* more productive? Do staff assume they need to work faster, setting aside quality? If your customer service staff, programmers, or project managers track project time, is unnecessary work performed? Are time logs padded? Do they assume they need 2,000 hours of billable time a year to get a raise?

Might your commissioned sales reps sell customers what they don't need or want just to meet their quota or earn a bonus? Do you have a policy of not giving credits, either stated or implied, that leaves staff with no viable solution for frustrated customers?

Last, consider billing. What message do your invoices send? Are they easy to understand? Can your staff explain every charge in a way that makes sense to customers? Are you billing surcharges and blaming it on outside forces?

Yes, there may be sound business reasons for each task that you measure. These practices can leave your business stronger and on a firmer financial footing, but there's also a risk. Take care in measuring business success. Be astute and pragmatic—from the customer's perspective—to produce the results you want.

Customer Service Success Tip

Make sure that what you measure and pay employees to do balances your business's financial goals with what's in your customers' best interest.

Even better, strive to keep customers happy. That's the best way to maintain a viable business.

Penny Wise and Dollar Foolish

Customer Service Failure Exists in Both Big and Small Ways

After moving from one town to another, I continued working with my long-time business accountant. Though most of our interactions occurred over the phone and through email, I persisted in making an hour-long trek to his office each tax season.

This was in part because of loyalty, but also my enjoyment in working with him. Another issue was inertia. Would searching for and finding a local replacement be an arduous task? Would the results be better or worse than my current situation?

Assets

On the plus side, my accountant was always available to answer my questions without charging me. I liked him as a person, identified with him as a business owner, and respected him as an accountant. Over the years, we had gotten to know each other, approaching a basic friendship.

Liabilities

The negative side of the ledger contained a few items as well. Besides handling my annual corporate and personal tax returns, one of my accountant's associates also processed my payroll. Though my requirements were as simple as possible, my needs sometimes caused my assigned contact to stumble.

I'd catch her errors. She'd apologize and correct them. But it's worrisome when the untrained person who doesn't do payroll uncovers a mistake made by the trained professional who does. These problems occurred each time a new person began working on my account, which happened every few years. Occasional issues popped up in between. If I changed firms, would my new selection be better or worse?

The second frustration, although trivial, caused more irritation. As companies migrated to emailing invoices and statements, my accounting firm persisted in mailing them. As the number of mailed invoices decreased, I ended up with only two folders in my accounts receivable file. One was for my accountant and the other for the United States Postal Service, which has an understandable interest in persisting to mail documents.

If my accountant missed this simple business trend, were there other things he was out of touch with too? This question gnawed at me, reinforced by each quarter's mailed invoice.

The third and most trivial issue shouldn't be worthy of mention, but I couldn't let it go. Each year, after completing my tax return, I'd receive a call from his office to come and pick up my forms and records. If I wanted them mailed, there was an additional charge—first six dollars and later ten.

Though my accountant said he would mail it at no cost, this information never made it to his frontline people. Each year when I complained about the fee, they'd sigh and place me on hold to confer with him.

They'd return to the phone sometime later to confirm they would waive the charge. This came forth as a resigned concession, as if I were taking money out of their own pocket. Never once was there an apology. Never did they show respect for me as their customer.

After a few years of this, I grew tired of asking and paid the fee, albeit with growing disdain.

Since I was driving an hour to see them and an hour back home just to continue using their services, I felt the least they could do was mail my paperwork to me at no cost. They could have even padded my bill by ten dollars, and I wouldn't have cared. But to announce the cost with a separate line item every year rumbled in my gut.

I paid them well over $1,000 each year. Charging me $10 to use their services was an insult. As I considered the rates I paid, I often wondered if they were competitive.

Restore the Balance

After six years of this long-distance accounting arrangement, it was time to change, to find a local provider, regardless of how difficult the transition might be. Turns out it was quite simple. My daughter-in-law recommended the firm she used for her business. Though her line of work is quite different from mine, our accounting needs are identical.

Based on her recommendation, I interviewed her CPA and hired him. Currently, he handles my taxes, and a junior CPA in his firm does my payroll. I've never questioned her work, and, as a bonus, she's easier to work with and provides a higher level of service than my prior accountant's associates.

The overall service level with my new accountant is higher, and the rates are lower. And there are no more mailing charges to irk me. Though my former accountant may have had a business reason to bill and track mailing fees as a separate line item, it served as an irritant that drove me away.

Customer Service Success Tip

Search for business practices that might make sense from your standpoint but alienate customers. Eliminate those items to better keep their business. You'll come out ahead in the end.

Consistency Matters Most

Tell Your Customers What to Expect and
Deliver it Every Time

Moving required finding a new place to service my car. A well-maintained auto repair business sat just down the street from our home, less than half a mile away. A neighbor, though he had never gone there, said they had a reputation for providing great service.

An Unexpected Twist

Before I could try them, however, another garage in the area mailed me a welcome-to-the-neighborhood coupon for a free oil change. This was a brilliant marketing move on their part. I figured I'd use the coupon and then try out the closer business, hopeful for them to become my provider of preference.

Though the second facility wasn't as near, they were still only a couple miles away. They, too, had a nice facility—newer, larger, and more impressive than the one down the street.

I called for my free oil change, and everything proceeded as expected. New filter, fresh oil, and no bill. As a bonus, they performed a courtesy check of my car and offered a few suggestions for recommended maintenance. Their explanation of the additional work sounded reasonable.

I later dropped my car off for part two. It cost me a couple hundred dollars this time, but I accepted it as normal for an aging car.

They impressed me with how they integrated technology into their operation, not only to service my car but also to interact with me. Despite having paid them over $200 for what I had planned to be a free oil change, I left pleased with their service and the outcome. In short, they delighted me.

Inconsistent Service

When our other car needed work, it was easy to return there—albeit not as convenient as going down the street. Again, they did their work as promised and met my expectations. Again, they had a list—this time longer—of additional work that they deemed urgent. This time the estimate was much higher. The explanation seemed less convincing. I walked away, not as happy, with the bill of several hundred dollars and only half the recommended work done.

Yet I returned the next time I had an auto-repair need.

They allowed me to schedule my appointments online, an option I appreciated given that I seldom remember to make my car repair appointments during business hours. Each time I booked my appointment, they asked for my preferred contact method: phone, text message, or email.

The first time I selected text message, but they called me instead. I figured it was an error on their part and overlooked it—mostly. From then on, I always selected email, but they persisted in calling. Once, when I didn't answer, they followed up with a text. Never once did they email me as requested.

Another time I dropped my car off for repair and, not needing it back for at least a month (and causing me to wonder if my family really needed a second car), I told them there was no rush. "Just email me when you're finished."

A week went by and then two with no email (or phone call or text). Then a third week with no communication. Then a tersely worded letter arrived. If I didn't pick up my car within 24 hours, they would charge me for storage. I went in, paid my bill, and retrieved my car.

I asked why they never contacted me about the completed repair. Their aloof customer service person offered no explanation, only a shoulder shrug.

I grew tired of going there. My first concern was that they always found something else to do. Too often I questioned the validity of their recommendations. Though they delighted me at first, they never repeated that feat. Instead, they provided mediocre service. This produced disappointment, such as not calling me in the manner requested or threatening to charge me to store the car I didn't know was ready for pickup.

Aside from aggressive recommendations for additional work on my cars, their actual repairs were good. But the inconsistent nature of our interactions led me to seek a different alternative. Not knowing what to expect each time I interacted with them led me to disappointment most of the time. I knew they could delight me because they did once. Why couldn't they accomplish that every time?

I gave up on them and, after much too long, contacted the garage down the street for my next oil change.

Consistent Service

Upon arriving, the customer service manager greeted me with an engaging smile. She entered my information in the computer and made my appointment. I dropped the car off as planned, picked it up when promised, and paid the bill I expected.

Though nothing was exceptional with our interaction, it was decidedly better than average. After my recent experiences with the other garage, above average excited me. I returned. Again and again.

Every time I had an above average experience. Each time I looked forward to my next visit. They were that good. They provided me with consistently above average interactions. I appreciated knowing what to expect and receiving it every time.

Their predictable service pleased me. They didn't delight me just once and then disappoint. They thrilled me on every visit.

I still take my vehicles there. I know that each time I take my car in I'll receive quality work, a fair bill with no surprises, and reasonable recommendations for possible additional work. I rate my interaction with them as consistently above average—and that's high praise.

I don't recall another auto repair facility ever being this predictable. With certainty, none were consistently above average. Even a garage consistently average would surpass most of my combined experiences at other service facilities, where they seldom followed one good encounter with a second.

Too often my auto-repair experiences were like a roller coaster: up and down. I never knew what to expect. And unlike roller coasters where surprises thrill riders, being surprised doesn't bode well for car repair.

Consistency is the key for ongoing success. This will earn you repeat business, time after time, year after year.

Customer Service Success Tip

Before you strive to improve your customer service, first aim to be consistent. This means uncovering the experiences that disappoint and eliminating them. Continue to address the low outliers to increase consistency in the remaining interactions.

Telephone Customer Service

The second of our three arenas of customer service interaction occurs over the telephone. When it isn't practical to interact in person, picking up the telephone is an ideal way to accomplish the customer service goal quickly and effectively. This, of course, hinges on the skill and ability of the person who answers the call. This may be a receptionist, a representative (or rep for short), or call center agent. But regardless of the title, the essential role they play in customer service satisfaction is identical.

While a trend, especially among younger consumers, is to go online to answer questions and resolve customer support issues, a call center, when done right, will surpass self-service every time.

We'll start our exploration with telephone basics and go from there.

~

The Trials and Triumphs of Telephone Support

Phone Interactions Can Save or
Ruin Your Business

A lot of customer service occurs over the telephone. This growing trend leaves me concerned about some things and excited about others.

A Shortsighted Attitude

On the negative side, consider a large telecommunications company that provides cell phone, internet, and long distance. Or a large national banking institution. You've heard of them both. And they're notorious for their abysmal record of poor customer service.

If I shared their names, there's a good chance you or someone you know has had an unpleasant experience with them. To call it *unpleasant* is kind. Uncaring, unconscionable, and unethical are more accurate characterizations.

With these companies, once a nontypical problem occurs, there's a strong likelihood they'll *never* resolve it. This isn't an overstatement. People have only so much patience. Then they give up. Excessive runaround, time spent on hold, and limited energy to pursue a satisfactory resolution end up overwhelming frustrated customers. They accept the problem or switch providers.

Although some of these companies' frontline staff care and try their best, too many do not. Regardless, there seems to be cumbersome bureaucracy thwarting every move and complex support systems that make no allowances for nonroutine problems.

A Solution for Success

There's an opportunity awaiting these two companies—and others like them—if they can just provide effective telephone customer service. With best-in-class phone support, their cancellation rates would plummet, and customer satisfaction levels would skyrocket. They'd receive a lot less negative press.

Are these companies simply too big or do they offer too many services to be effective? Are their help desks mismanaged, bogged down by bureaucracy, or smothered with complexity?

I suspect the underlying reason is that upper management treats support as an expense to minimize. But exemplary customer service is good business. Investing in customer support is an investment in your future.

A Positive Outcome

I experienced the trials and triumphs of phone support after my house took a minor lightning strike.

The surge affected our phone, internet, and entertainment services. I called my satellite provider and spoke with Beth in the Oklahoma call center. This was the first time I encountered a call center agent telling me her location. It seemed hokey and an overreaction to the backlash against offshore call centers, but it helped me establish a personal connection with Beth from Oklahoma.

While waiting for various diagnostics to run, we had time to chat, which I enjoyed and found preferable to sitting in silence on hold. She soon scheduled a service call for the next day. The technician fixed the problem fast and restored service.

I wish I could say the same for my phone and internet service providers. They both required multiple phone calls. Then there were the missed commitments, wrong instructions, and conflicting information.

That's no way to run a business.

Customer Service Success Tip

Listen to what customers say about your service. Then do one thing to improve it. Once complete, fix the next item on the list.

Call Center 101

Understand Call Center Basics Before Moving Forward

I once consulted with call centers. I'd often receive phone calls and emails from people who wanted to start a call center. At first, I invested time with them, hoping for a paid assignment. I'd discuss the nuances, ramifications, and challenges of starting a call center. But this never produced a paying client.

After too many such calls, I developed a shortcut to gauge their level of industry understanding, saving myself from wasting time. I'd ask them two questions.

The first question was, "Will your call center do inbound or outbound work?" This confused many people. One person, who claimed fifteen years of call center experience, responded with, "What do you mean? I don't understand the difference."

My second question was, "Will this be an in-house or an outsource call center?" This query generated even more confusion. "What?" one caller gasped. "We're in the United States!"

If you see a call center in your organization's future, this primer will answer some initial questions and minimize confusion.

Inbound Call Centers

Inbound call centers answer calls. It's that simple. Their agents are in a reactive mode, waiting for the phone to ring or the next call in queue. They don't make calls.

Inbound centers have ACDs (automatic call distributors). ACDs route calls to the "next available agent." It's most efficient.

Many inbound operations operate 24/7. They schedule agents around the clock to meet the expected number of calls based on historical data and marketing initiatives.

Outbound Call Centers

Outbound call centers make calls to customers and sales prospects. Their job is proactive. Even if agent work is not sales per se, they still need a sales mentality. They must engage the called party, lead them toward an objective, and deal with rejection—which happens often. Some rebuffs they receive may attack them as a person.

Most modern outbound call centers rely on computerized dialers to automatically place calls for their staff. Managers schedule agents as needed to complete a required number of calls within a certain window of time, as allowed by law.

There are two types of outbound calling.

The first, which irritates most people, is calling individuals at home or on their cell phone to sell them a product or promote an initiative. This is a business calling to a consumer or B2C for short. Because of past over calling and abuse, most aspects of B2C outbound work face strict regulations, with violators subject to stiff fines for noncompliance. As a result, most B2C calling now focuses on consumers that have an existing business relationship with the company.

The other type of outbound work is one business calling another business, known as B2B. Though less regulated, businesses placing outbound calls to other businesses must still exercise care when doing so.

Hybrid Call Centers

Though not as common, hybrid call centers do both inbound and outbound work. Their basic function might seem the same, but from a practical standpoint, they function as independent operations. This is because few agents can switch with ease between the two types of calls.

In-house Call Centers

An in-house call center is an internal department or division of a business. Some call it a corporate call center. It provides services only for their own company. The advantages of having an internal call center are greater control of the operation, its agents, and their activities.

An in-house call center can be a cost-center or a profit-center. As cost-centers, they do not generate enough revenue to cover their operational expenses. The company must subsidize their operation. In contrast, a call center that operates as a profit-center generates revenue. They cover their operational expenses and produce a profit for their company. They often do this through sales and customer retention.

Outsource Call Centers

An outsource call center works for other companies. Their business is receiving calls (inbound) or making calls (outbound). They often enjoy an economy-of-scale that is not possible to achieve with an in-house operation. As such, their margins allow their clients to *save* money while they *make* money.

Agents at an outsource call center work with their clients' customers or prospects. Outsource call centers are increasing in number and importance. This is because more companies seek outsourcing to increase service levels and options, return to their core competencies, save money, or all three.

When outsourcing telephone communication, it's critical to choose a reputable, quality-focused partner. Since they will function as an extension of your business, carefully vet them to select a provider that will represent you well. Make your decision based on maximizing positive outcomes and not just curtailing costs.

Offshore Call Centers

An offshore call center is any call center that operates in a different country, that is, offshore. Both in-house and outsource call centers can move offshore.

Too often, however, people equate offshoring with outsourcing. They are not the same thing. Offshore call centers can be a subset of the outsourcing call center industry. Yet an in-house call center can move offshore as well.

Several years ago, the trend was to move call center activity to other countries that boasted stable technological infrastructures and offered qualified workers who possessed lower wage expectations. This is offshoring.

In recent years, however, many offshore call center operations have moved back to their home country. This happened because the expected benefits did not materialize, and a customer backlash occurred against hard-to-understand, foreign-sounding agents, many who were not using their native tongue at work.

Summary

Categorize your call center or call center plans in terms of these definitions to better understand its function and manage its operation. The key reason to do so is that call centers provide a key communications channel that is both effective and affordable when compared to alternatives.

Customer Service Success Tip

Even if you don't think you have a call center, you do have a telephone. Learn all you can about call centers and apply this knowledge to your operation, regardless of its size.

The Truth About Interactive Voice Response

*Most IVR Systems Cause More Customer
Service Issues Than They Address*

Interactive voice response (IVR) seems to be everywhere—and no one likes it. You call a company and get a recording. Who wants that? In response to infuriating IVR systems that give endless levels of confusing options, many callers seek to bypass the machine by pressing zero—often many times—to reach a person.

Sometimes this works. Sometimes it doesn't.

The Wrong Approach

If a company has no regard for its customers, then they should expand their IVR system. Force callers to spend more time interacting with a machine so their employees will spend less time interacting with callers. They should do everything possible to keep customers from talking to staff. This will hold costs down and make their operation look good from a financial standpoint.

This is fine if they have a captive customer base, operate a monopoly, or assume it's easier to get a new customer than to keep an existing one (it's not). Otherwise, they need to listen with care to what the buying public is saying, because, in this case, the customer is right.

The Right Application

IVR has its place in business, but we must not overstate what that place is. If IVR can speed up the call for the customer or gather information that can help an employee provide better, more effective service, then use an IVR.

However, when the primary goal of IVR becomes saving money, reducing the employee headcount, or limiting customer service options, then the intent is shortsighted.

If your company uses an IVR, consider these recommendations:

IVR Dos

- Always provide an option for the caller to press 0 to talk to a person.

- Provide short and basic options that someone from outside your organization can understand.

- Ask friends to call and test your IVR. Then fix the things that bug or confuse them.

- Consider how you would want the ideal IVR to run. Then set up your company's IVR that way.

IVR Don'ts

- Don't block the digit 0. If a customer wants to talk to a person, let them.

- Don't prompt for an account number if the operator will ask for it again.

- Don't have callers enter their selection (such as "billing") and then not route them to billing or let the agent know which option they picked.

- Don't route callers to a general-purpose call center agent after the caller just took the time to tell the IVR why they're calling. Skip this wasted step and just route the call.

- Don't provide level after level of long menu options. Keep the options short and simple.

- Don't force an already irritated customer to go through a lengthy and cumbersome IVR tree, because they will exit it more annoyed, venting their frustration to your staff.

For most companies, their IVR doesn't work as it should and needs attention.

Customer Service Success Tip

Evaluate your IVR system with an open mind and then fix its problems.

Does Anyone Like Speech Recognition?

Ensure that Technology Helps and Doesn't Hinder True Customer Service

I'm a fan of technology. The allure of computers understanding and reacting to spoken words excites me. Yet real-life implementations often overflow with frustration-producing moments. Although now better than earlier versions, speech recognition still lacks in providing customer service.

In the past I've been wary to state my disappointment with speech recognition, knowing that I'm part of the problem: my words often lack clarity. That doesn't make the software's job any easier.

A Failure to Communicate

Some errors come from imprecise speech, such as asking for Candy Lane and ending up with Cam Delain. Other occurrences are nonsensical, making for a great comedy skit, albeit poor customer service. For example:

"Good morning, Acme Call Center; your call is important to us. Please say the department or name of the person you are calling."

"Sally Pavasaris," I say.

"Did you say Ned Flanders?"

"No!"

Nothing happens.

"Sal-ee-Pa-va-sar-is," I project in my best diction.

"I'm sorry, I don't understand. Please say the department or name of the person you are calling."

"Agent!" I beg. "Operator!" I shout.

I press zero with repeated vigor. When I'm at last connected to a person, my demeanor is less than ideal.

I know why, but the agent is clueless, likely muttering about rude customers after she ends my call.

To further complicate matters, what if I don't know the person's full name? What if I can't pronounce their last name? Speech recognition struggles with such situations.

When to Speak and When to Listen

Another common issue that I have is knowing how to proceed when the software and I talk at the same time. A common dilemma is:

"Please say your account number."

"Seven," I begin.

". . . followed by the pound sign," the voice continues.

I now have a critical decision. Do I assume it recognized my "seven," allowing me to proceed in giving the rest of my account number? Or should I repeat the first digit? If I guess wrong, I'll waste more time attempting fruitless communication with a machine.

Either way, I'm apt to hear, "I'm sorry. That number is invalid. Please try again."

Sometimes I try to suppress my impatient tendencies. (Why am I more patient with people than machines?) I wait to make sure the voice has finished talking. Yet I may delay too long, at which point I'm rewarded with an unwelcome reprimand. "Please respond now."

To avoid causing the voice further frustration, I comply. This causes the situation I tried to avoid in the first place, with the machine and me talking at the same time. At this point things spiral further out of control.

The software still doesn't know my account number, I still don't know when to speak and when to listen, and I'm sensing that the likelihood of talking *with* an actual person—versus talking *to* a machine trying to act like a person—is even more unlikely than when I started the call.

Focus on Customer Outcomes

A good speech recognition solution can speed up call processing and improve caller satisfaction. But that goal often goes unrealized. Instead, expensive implementation attempts produce little—aside from frustrated customers and maligned customer service personnel.

Technology must produce better outcomes, for both your customers and your staff.

Customer Service Success Tip

Interact with your company's automation as a customer or prospect would. Even better, hire an outsider to be a secret shopper. Prioritize frustrations and failures. Then fix them.

The Perfect Answer

*Learn the Ideal Way to Greet Callers and
Make a Great Impression*

How often have you called a company and wondered if you reached the right number? Busy employees too often answer phone calls in a rush, causing callers to wonder what they said. Or the receptionist gasps for breath after spitting out a lengthy, tongue-twisting greeting.

An equally important consideration is for everyone at an organization to answer every call the same way.

There are three parts to the ideal way to answer the phone:

1. Opening

Begin with a social pleasantry. Just say "Good morning," "Good afternoon," or "Good evening." During the holiday season, "Happy holidays" or "Season's greetings" are options. The opening tells the caller that you have answered the phone, and that it's time for them to listen.

If the caller lacks focus or needs to adjust his or her ears to catch your phrasing, pace, or accent, the opening gives time for this to happen, since it isn't critical if missed. Last, these first words set a positive tone for the call.

2. Company Identity

The second phrase is the name of your business or organization, such as, "Acme Industries." It lets callers know who they've reached, confirming they dialed the right number.

In most cases, state your company name as people outside your organization would say it. This means dropping legal suffixes, such as Inc., LLC, and Ltd., or other formal elements that would confuse the caller rather than clarify.

For the same reason, don't shorten or abbreviate the company name, either. To answer with "AI" when everyone knows you as "Acme Industries" helps no one.

3. Your Name

The last element is the employee's first name. This provides a valuable personal connection. It's much easier for a caller to get mad at an anonymous voice than an actual person who has a name. Giving your name allows you to build a rapport with the caller.

As the last word of your greeting, it's also the one best remembered by the caller. Omitting your name implies a lack of interest. Ending with your name signals accessibility. This is essential in problem-solving and customer service situations.

Avoid Unnecessary Additions

It's all too common for people to tack on the ridiculous phrase, "How may I direct your call?" A literal response to this senseless question is "fast and correctly." This is not effective communication. Drop pointless embellishments.

Put these elements together to result in the perfect answer:

"Good morning, Acme Industries, this is Peter."

Related Tips

The person answering must give their full attention to the caller, being ready to listen. They should have pen and paper nearby to jot quick notes. This avoids making the caller repeat information.

Customer Service Success Tip

Call your organization to see what happens. Then instruct your staff on the right way to answer your phone. Make sure everyone follows it.

One Moment While I Disconnect Your Call

Aim for 100 Percent Success When Transferring Callers

The success rate of customer service staff transferring calls is not good. Though they're doing better now than they once did, they can still improve. I expect complete success. This isn't unreasonable.

Consider my all-too-frequent experience:

The person who answers attempts to transfer my call. But I hear no ringing. There's no music on hold. I don't know what happened or what to expect.

As I wait in silence, I suspect my call will soon come to a premature end. A return to dial tone confirms this. Or a recording tells me to "hang up and try your call again." This confirms they disconnected me. Although this could result from a technical issue, a much more probable cause is human error.

When a disconnected caller calls back, how has their mood changed? Regardless of their initial attitude when they first called, they are now less pleased. The person they talk to unjustly receives their understandable ire.

None of these outcomes are necessary, and the additional stress to agents on subsequent calls is unwarranted. You can tip the odds in your favor by following some basic, but often overlooked, steps:

Train

Employee training must cover proper transfer procedure. For some phone systems, transferring a call is a straightforward process, while other platforms require a complex string of button pushing or mouse clicking.

During training, the trainee should experience the call transfer from three different perspectives. One is the caller being transferred. The second is the employee making the handoff. The third is the person receiving the call.

Too often, the person who transfers the call never experiences the process from the caller's or the recipient's perspective. But doing so gives them a better understanding of how errors affect others. This provides some much-needed empathy.

Practice

To master a skill requires practice. Perform it until it becomes rote. Ample practice should occur prior to attempting it with a real caller. In addition, when using phone systems with more complex transferring procedures, staff who rarely transfer calls should have ongoing practice.

Consistency

Most telephone systems provide multiple ways to transfer calls. Pick the most applicable method and teach it to all employees. Have trainers explain this standard method and no others. Keep receptionists from using different methods or seeking shortcuts.

Don't let them share non-approved methods with others. When they do, problems will result.

Method

Decide on one philosophy for transferring calls.

A *blind transfer* is the quickest but least professional. With it the employee calls the extension or dials the number, connects the caller to the ringing line, and hangs up before anyone answers. Although common, it's not even close to "best practice," as this requires the caller to repeat the reason for their call.

In an *announced transfer*, the employee dials the number and waits for the called party to answer. They tell the recipient about the call, connect the caller, and then hang up.

A *confirmed transfer* is one step beyond an announced transfer. In this method, the receptionist stays connected long enough to ensure that the recipient can address the caller's needs. Once the first rep confirms this, they hang up.

However, if the called employee cannot help the caller, then the first employee can retake control of the call and transfer it to the correct person. This eliminates audio quality degradation that can occur when transferring a call a second time and even a third time.

This method also lets the first person know they sent the caller to the wrong person or department. Without this knowledge, the employee is apt to continue to repeat this same mistake.

Verification

Check transfer lists from time to time. This doesn't mean to just review the information but to dial each number. Over time, directories become outdated. Frequent verification is the only sure way to confirm that employees have accurate information. A slower time of the day or week is an ideal occasion to assign an employee to test each number on the transfer list.

Lest you write this off as too time consuming or not cost-effective, consider the price of dealing with an irate caller who calls back after a careless employee routed them to the wrong number or cut them off. Even worse, what if they never call back?

First-Call Resolution

Resolving issues on the first call removes the need to transfer callers. First-call resolution (FCR) is the best prescription of all.

Customer Service Success Tip

Implement consistent call-transfer training. Have agents practice. Verify transfer lists and call directories.

Even better, pursue first-call resolution, and remove the need to transfer callers.

Your Staff on Autopilot

*Do Your Employees Think about Their Work
or Work Without Thinking?*

I once called Visa with an inquiry about my statement. A knowledgeable and professional rep answered my question. After an effective call, he concluded by saying, "Thank you for calling American Express."

Shocked, I said nothing. Either he didn't realize what he had uttered or cringed that he had stated the wrong company name. Regardless, his mouth was on autopilot and his mind, disengaged. Seeking to avoid causing him embarrassment, I said, "You're welcome," and hung up.

In contemplating this, I wondered if he had just changed jobs, moving from American Express to Visa. More likely he worked for a credit card outsource call center, which handled calls for both Visa and AmEx, and he had given the wrong credit card company name.

Or I suppose he could have been bored and wanted to see how people responded to his miscommunication. Stranger things have happened.

The Result of Repetition

Many jobs, including call center work, involve a great deal of repetition that occurs in quick succession. It's no wonder employees switch to autopilot and cruise through their day without thinking. Even the best workers can succumb to this, while uncaring ones subsist in this mode. As a result, we can expect a certain percentage of customer communication to flow forth without any thought. Though it's no excuse, is it any wonder that mistakes occur?

The situation worsens when a metrics-motivated manager pushes staff to work faster and process more transactions per hour. The result is staff thinking about the next customer before they've finished helping the current one.

Wrong Wrap-Ups

Another amusing autopilot trap frequently happens at the end of a customer service interaction. It's when an employee asks, "Is there anything else I can help you with today?" Often this is appropriate. It ensures they've addressed all the customer's concerns. Sometimes, however, asking this question is nonsensical, even infuriating.

One such unwarranted situation is when closing an account. I once called a company to cancel my service. I told the agent I was not happy with their product, that it didn't meet my expectations, and they could do nothing to resolve the problem. Though I tried to be polite, I suspect I was terse.

After an apology and some subsequent typing, the agent announced she'd canceled my account. Then she asked, "Is there anything else I can help you with today?"

What else might there be?

I won't open an account—I just closed one. I don't want to place an order, I'm not happy with the service, and I am no longer a customer. What else might she help me with? Nothing—so why ask?

Another scenario occurred when calling with a question. After trying to help, but without success, the rep apologized for her inability to address my concern. Then she asked, "Is there anything else I can help you with today?"

I wanted to scream. "You didn't help me with my first item, so how could you help me with anything else?" The only thing accomplished by asking this question in the wrong situation is to waste my time and theirs.

Some call center managers, however, may object. "Our agents aren't on autopilot. It's our policy to say this on every call."

To which I ask, "Why?"

Turning Off Autopilot

It's easy to see why staff slip into autopilot. It's hard to keep them working with intention or move them back to it once they've left.

Intentional work starts with training. Teach employees to focus on the moment, to view each caller in isolation. Encourage staff to concentrate on that caller and only that caller. This will help agents to address the customer's reason for calling fully and without distraction. Don't encourage them to cut the call short because there are calls in queue or to race through each interaction to achieve a statistical goal.

This brings us to call center metrics. If you focus on numeric speed and efficiency results, that's what you can expect to achieve. Instead, emphasize service outcomes. Look at increasing first-call resolution, minimizing callbacks, and improving customer satisfaction.

While you may never fully stop autopilot from occurring, you can minimize it.

Customer Service Success Tip

Employee autopilot can occur in any repetitive job, ranging from customer service to manufacturing to clerical. Seek ways to move staff from autopilot to intentional work. They're apt to like their jobs more. And the positive outcomes of their work will soar.

Guilty Until Proven Innocent

Key Lessons in Customer Support

When my internet service goes down, I seldom call customer support to report it—at least not anymore. I don't have the time to waste with my provider's nonsensical troubleshooting process. Instead, I wait in hopes someone else will report the outage and achieve a timely resolution.

This hasn't always been my approach. When I first had internet service, I would dutifully call customer service at the first sign of an outage.

Their agents' poor customer service skills and lengthy queries, however, left me frustrated. Their staff treated me as though the problem were my fault. They proceeded on the assumption they could restore service by having me reprogram my computer.

Asking me to reconfigure my computer or modem months after installation is ludicrous—and insulting.

Here's what usually happens:

Agents operate on the assumption that I'm guilty until proven innocent. They force me to invest up to an hour of my time checking many things before they'll take a trouble ticket. This escapes my comprehension. Even more astounding is that apologizing for an outage isn't part of their protocol.

To compound the situation, in the process of "troubleshooting," they instruct me to make many changes, which might leave me unable to connect to the internet once they correct the system outage. Never once have they given any instructions for returning my computer to its original configuration. They even neglect to suggest that I make note of the original settings so that I can restore them later. Fortunately, I now know better.

In a monopoly environment, this indifferent attitude would be understandable, albeit unacceptable. But I have options and will select the provider that irritates me the least. Notice I didn't say a provider with excellent service, or that delights me, or that has first-call resolution. My customer service expectations with internet service companies are so low that I merely desire to minimize my annoyance.

Though the above examples come from internet companies, I've had the same experiences with my telephone company (back when I had a landline), entertainment provider, and computer support vendor.

Regardless of the industry, here are a few commonsense ideas that every company should follow.

Take Responsibility

The agents I talked to acted as though their network, system, or product was impervious to failure and that the blame lay with me. Even if the customer is at fault, agents should reach this conclusion with care, assuming the problem is on their end until they determine the opposite.

Isolate the Problem

The *final* troubleshooting step the agents perform on my internet service is to connect to my modem. This should be the *first* test. If they can connect and run diagnostics, then the issue is probably on my end. If they can't access the modem, there's no need to harass me with needless tests and counterproductive repro-gramming on my end.

Though this recommendation doesn't readily translate to all businesses, look for quick ways to de-lineate between user issues and provider problems. Then target the troubleshooting in the right area.

Apologize

It's easy to say, "I'm sorry you're experiencing prob-lems." But too often this commonsense empathy nev-er occurs—or happens begrudgingly, as through grit-ted teeth.

Use Customer Relationship Management Software

If they had a functional customer service database (called a customer relationship management or CRM system), the agents would know that *every* time I called it was because of an outage. That *never* once have I called because of a problem on my end. They should know I have a history of being credible and not wasting their time—even though they have a history of wasting mine.

A good CRM system should be the backbone of any large-scale support effort. The next step is getting staff to use it, both to enter existing support details and to review past interactions.

Customer Service Success Tip

Train technical customer service staff to respect customers' time and not assume they're at fault or stupid.

How to Handle Cancellations

*Reduce Customer Deflections with the Right
Approach at the Right Time*

I once signed up for a credit card because of its rewards package. Although I built up an impressive number of points, I never redeemed them. Over time, my priorities changed, and I realized I would never use them. I called to see what other options they offered. Was there another reward incentive I could switch to? Did they offer cash back? How about merchandise? Did they have other options?

The answers were "No," "No," "No," and "No."

"I guess my only option is to cancel the card," I ventured.

"Is that what you want?" the agent asked.

"Let me think about it." Though I wanted to cancel, I desired a controlled switch.

The Cancellation Call

It took a while, but I finally switched all uses for that card to another one. I called again, this time to terminate service. The person who answered transferred me to their cancellation department. This agent feigned shock at my intent to cancel. She tried to dissuade me. She offered a lower rate, better terms, and more flexibility on the rewards package.

Her options for a different rewards program would have kept me as a cardholder, except that she offered them too late. Having just spent several weeks getting ready to stop using this card, I intended to follow through. I canceled it.

Normal Operating Procedure

This scenario too often repeats. I've seen it with my cell phone, entertainment, long distance, and local phone service providers.

Each time the agents answering the phone lacked the authority, ability, or training to keep me as a customer. Each time I made careful plans, arranging for service from their competitor. When I called back to end my service, the cancellation department would step in and sweeten the deal. They'd often offer the concessions I wanted and which I suspected were available all along. But the frontline staff I talked to on my first calls never offered them.

These cancellation specialists would express regret over my decision and ask me to call back if I changed my mind. If only someone had offered these solutions earlier. Then they would have kept me as a customer and saved me the aggravation of switching.

Too Accommodating

The solution seemed obvious. Just pretend I'm going to cancel so I can reach the cancellation department on my first call and get their best deal. I tried that once. It went like this:

"I want to cancel my service."

"Oh, I'm sorry to hear that. Let me see what I can do."

I wait, expecting her to transfer me to a cancellation specialist. After a few seconds, the agent announces, "Okay, I canceled your service. Is there anything else I can help you with?"

I was too embarrassed to say I didn't want to cancel. I thanked her and hung up.

Conclusion

In the first examples, the staff trained and empowered to keep me as a customer came too late into the process. At that point, I'd made my decision and put the alternative in place. My call was a mere formality to end our business relationship.

In the last scenario, the agent possessed the authority and ability to handle a cancellation call, but she lacked training. She was efficient but ineffective.

How does your company handle cancellations? Do you empower all staff to process terminations, with ease and without hassle? Or do you have a specific cancellation strategy, with a team assigned and trained to follow an exact protocol?

Either approach has its strengths and limitations, but both can fall short of the customer's best interest.

Customer Service Success Tip

Train and empower employees at your company to interact with unhappy customers while there is still a reasonable chance to keep them.

A Well-Timed Call Can Make All the Difference

Overcome an Epic Customer Service Failure
with Appropriate Follow-Up

On the same day, I experienced both poor customer service and great customer service. Both came from the same organization.

By choice, I use a local bank. My bank has a home office and two branches. For twelve years, I've always used the same branch.

Once, I went online to check on a transaction—or at least I attempted to. Login denied. Next, I tried bank-by-phone. Invalid password.

Last I called their home office to find out about the transaction.

Training Shortfall

Though the woman who answered understood my request, she took several minutes to find the information I needed. Lengthy hold times were part of the process. Once accomplished, she was about to hang up when I stopped her.

"I can't log in to online banking or bank-by-phone." I gave her the details. Once she realized I wished to resolve these issues, she put me on hold again.

It's Your Fault

She returned, telling me what to do when I've forgotten my password.

"I didn't forget it," I clarified. "It's just not working."

She did some typing and conferred with her co-worker, this time without putting me on hold. Their exchange was most entertaining.

My situation confused her. She instructed me to try again. When that didn't work, she said the system had locked me out because of too many failed login attempts.

"But I was just doing what you told me to do."

You Have To

There was more conferring with her coworker. Her next words jarred me. "To reset your password, you *have to* send in written authorization." She wouldn't help me until I did.

"That is most disappointing," I replied and ended the call.

This was not my first customer service nightmare that day. I began griping to myself. "I don't have to do anything. It'll be faster to cancel my accounts than to send in a written request."

Though switching banks might have been satisfying from an emotional standpoint, it was not practical.

Make It Right

I was still stewing when the phone rang. It was the manager at my local branch. We're on a first-name basis. She apologized for her coworker's poor communication.

For security, the bank had required every customer to change their passwords. They would block our access until we complied. To address the deluge of phone calls that resulted, they hired the person I talked to. But I doubt they had time to provide much training.

In the few seconds it took to explain this, the manager had reset my password, and I could log in again. We would deal with the paperwork later.

The manager's exemplary response overcame the disappointing shortcomings of her coworker. It was an ideal example of customer service recovery.

Customer Service Success Tip

A timely placed phone call can make all the difference between losing and keeping a customer. Encourage your staff to pass on the names of customers who might need a follow-up call. Thank the employee for the information and don't punish them. Then call that customer.

Online and Multichannel Customer Service

The third area of customer service interactions happens online. This may occur in self-service situations, interacting with the customer service bot, or through the help of a person via text chat or email.

Online customer service seldom occurs in isolation, however, often preceding or following in-person interaction or telephone communications. This means some situations switch between all three. This reminds us that customer service—especially when online support is part of the mix—does not exist in one place or occur in one way but shifts from one channel to another as a consumer moves along their customer journey.

Available and Accurate Support

Minimizing the Need for Customer Service Is the Best Support Option

As an author, I upload my books to over a half-dozen online stores and distributors, using their respective portals to enter each book's information and files. The interface for each one differs, with some being easy to use and others being more cumbersome. Sometimes it's clear what information they seek, and other sites provide on-page tips to answer essential questions.

Each one of these online destinations offers a degree of customer support.

Questionable Results

One online bookseller, the oldest of them all, has a confusing-to-navigate website that leaves users questioning what information to enter. They offer both email and telephone support, though experience encourages me to use these options only as a last resort—and then to question the results. Given the quality of communication that occurs through both options, I assume these reps are in a different country, one far removed from mine.

I'd be fine with this if they were easier to understand, and I trusted what they told me. Too often, however, I wonder about the accuracy of their answers. And when I really question the validity of their advice, I contact them a second time and receive a contradictory response. I don't recall ever getting the same answer twice.

Unavailable and Delayed

Another publishing vendor offers email and text chat support. They used to be most helpful and responsive. However, in the last year this has changed. Their text chat option is unavailable most of the time, turning on and off throughout the day. Checking during posted times of availability, I've twice seen that chat was online, but before I could enter my question, it went off-line.

I've now given up on even trying chat and use email instead. I measure their response time for email requests in weeks, not hours. The good part is that I respect their answers—at least most of the time.

Professional and Accurate

The other companies all offer just email support.

Two of them surpass all others—not only in the publishing industry but for all e-commerce companies. Though they don't meet my hope for a quick response, they do respond, usually by the next business day. What makes them excel, however, is the professionalism of their communications and the accuracy of their answers.

I fully trust what they tell me.

Follow the example of these two booksellers. Make sure that your online presence is easy for customers to use and offers accessible, helpful, on-page support. If you have customers or vendors who up-load information to your website, make sure the backend is equally easy to use and helpful.

Customer Service Success Tip

Make your e-commerce store easier to use, for both customers and vendors. Each improvement you make online will lessen the work your customer service support staff must do later.

Provider-Inflicted Pain

Balance Business Needs with
Customer Impact

It's a hassle when our credit card changes. We must track down every business that has our credit card number on file and update it. If we miss one company, we risk service interruptions or delivery problems.

Sometimes we decide to switch cards, but what about when our credit card company makes this change? Through no fault of our own, they force us to use a new card with a different number. This doesn't happen often, but I have experienced it with both my personal and business accounts.

The most recent occurrence happened to me with the branded card I used for all my business purchases. They aligned with a different credit card provider, and I paid the price for that decision. I'm sure it made sense for them, but did they consider how this would affect their customers?

The Personal Impact

The first to update were the companies that automatically charged my card each month. The process to correct this was straightforward, albeit time-consuming. I looked at last month's statement and listed everyone I needed to contact. Then I went online to provide my new credit card information. Though time-consuming and tedious, this step wasn't hard. Some sites made updating my credit card information easy, but other sites buried this information or made the process more challenging.

But what about all the companies that had my credit card number on file, but I hadn't bought from them in the last month? This list was much harder to compile, and I overlooked a few. But I didn't know I had missed them until I attempted to place an order and had my card denied—all because I forgot to update my number. This produced both frustration and embarrassment.

Business Decisions

Don't just evaluate business changes from a financial perspective. Consider how this will impact your customers. Will your decision inconvenience them or damage your relationship with them?

Though this example is about credit cards, the lesson applies elsewhere too. Other considerations include updating software, changing password requirements, and migrating from one system to another. Before proceeding, consider how these changes will impact your customers. Look for ways to mitigate their frustration or minimize their inconvenience.

Customer Service Success Tip

When you make a business decision, consider how it affects your customers. Seek ways to ease the transition for them. Consider what you can do for them, so that they won't have to do it themselves.

~

Customer Survey Failure

Poll Customers to Enhance—Not Harm—
Your Business Relationship

As a business, do you email surveys to your customers?

As a consumer, do you take part in customer surveys? Sometimes I do, and other times I don't. I'm not sure if they improve the service I receive or not. But completing them makes me feel better when I'm frustrated.

Based on my experiences, here are some insights about customer surveys, getting usable results, and providing notable service.

Don't Over-Survey Customers

My first encounter with a customer service survey gone awry was with an equipment vendor. I called them often, attempting to resolve several ongoing software problems with their system. Every call—even if the problem remained unresolved—generated a follow-up customer service survey. I completed each one, assuming I was doing my part to help them improve their processes and increase quality.

I was fair in my evaluations, giving high marks when earned and not so high ratings when warranted. But I *never* gave them a below average score.

Protect Respondent Identity

I assumed my responses were confidential.

Imagine my surprise when I met their staff at a convention a few months later. Over the course of the three-day event, no less than five people from that company, including the CEO, confronted me about my survey scores. They were all aware of the marks I had been giving them—and they were mad.

It seems I was lowering the curve. Each one claimed my "poor" responses hurt their evaluations. I assumed I was helping, but they didn't share my perspective. Instead, I made them angry. This wasn't improving my chances of receiving the help I needed when I called.

After their repeated rebukes, I never filled out another one of their surveys.

Survey All Customers, Not a Handpicked Few

I don't need to call my web hosting company often, but when I do, they're responsive and helpful. Most of the time, they resolve my issue on the first call. Sometimes, at the call's completion, they ask if they can email me a customer survey.

Most agents make this offer on easy calls with a positive outcome. But they don't do so after complicated conversations. By picking who to survey, they skew the results and receive only favorable feedback. Any conclusions drawn from the responses mean nothing.

Prohibit Survey Coaching

Several times, after my biannual switch of cell phone providers, I'm told to expect an automated customer service survey. Each time, the accommodating salesperson told me to respond with a five on every question. To do so would verify his service pleased me. Anything less would count against him.

This has happened with multiple carriers. It's also occurred in other industries. I doubt those looking at the survey results know their employees coach respondents to leave fives on every answer.

This makes the results meaningless.

Call Back in the Manner Requested

Once, after switching phone companies on my business line, I received a call from my old carrier. They left a message in voicemail about my reluctance to recommend them, as noted on my survey when I canceled service.

In this voicemail message, the caller asked that I call and leave a message with the best time and best number for them to reach me. I did, leaving my office number and asking for a return call on Monday.

Instead, they called my cell phone on Sunday, causing me further irritation by ignoring the information they asked for and I provided. The agent did not try to win me back or leave the door open for my return. He did, however, say with condescension that updating my service with them would have resolved my quality issues.

Leave Understandable Messages and Ensure Your Number Works

A week later, I received a welcome call from my new carrier. It was a person, not a recording. She called my office after hours and left a message. The fast-talking agent spewed forth her reason for calling, callback number, and an eleven-character identifier I was to give them on my return call. I played the message four times before I caught all the digits.

I dialed the number. It rang a couple of times. I received the typical "your call may be recorded" message, heard another ring, and then silence. Repeated calls produced the same result.

Out of curiosity, a few days later I tried again. A recording said, "At this time we are unable to answer your call. Please try your call again later."

I'll never know why they wanted me to call, but if they had sent me a survey, I'd remind them how important it is to make sure their phones are working when they ask me to call and that they should bother to answer when I do.

Summary

When surveying your customers, what is your intent? Are your practices and methods supporting that goal or thwarting it? If you follow up with a customer or former customer, make sure you strengthen the business relationship and not damage it.

Customer Service Success Tip

Evaluate the need to conduct surveys, how your employees view them, and if the data produces reliable, actionable results.

~

Service Sold It

Don't Talk about Providing Quality Service,
Just Do It

E xcept for retail, most companies today provide most of their service online, sometimes
backed by telephone support when needed.
Yet regardless of the channel—in person, over the
phone, or online—the common goal is (or should be)
to provide quality service to customers and better ensure their ongoing patronage.

As a child, I remember a radio commercial with
the tagline, "Service sold it." Even at an early age, I
knew that delivering quality service was the best path
to business success.

Over the years, I've heard this idea repeated
by many companies. Yet I now give it only passing
consideration. This phrase has a hollow ring. It's a

disingenuous assurance, holding an empty promise. What was once good business has merely become good ad copy. Consumers ignore it amid the clutter of promotions that they no longer believe.

In fact, the louder a business trumpets this claim, the less credence I give it, and the more I assume their quality falls short. Their ad campaign's only goal is to convince us of the contrary. To paraphrase George Bernard Shaw, "He who can, does. He who cannot, talks about it." Hardly anyone, it seems, provides quality service anymore. They just say they do.

As we continue our customer service journey, I'll dig back in time to unearth four lessons to frame our discussion.

Computer Company Failure

I once ordered some computers and accessories online. My order arrived, but there was a problem with one item. To correct the issue required great patience and much persistence. I endured long hold times, transfers to the wrong departments and back again, and reps who struggled with English. One humorous example was the man who said, "Excuse please the silence while I hold you."

To reach my goal, I had to escalate my call, invoke their "100 Percent Satisfaction Guarantee," and insist they accept the return of my *entire* order before they agreed to send me the one missing part.

It took a dozen phone calls over several weeks, but at last I received a satisfactory outcome. Based on this experience, however, I deemed their extended customer support plan would be a waste of money.

Telephone Company Failure

When phone companies first offered Caller ID, I ordered a feature that would display the number of a second caller while I talked to the first. It never worked. I called their repair number to report the problem. The rep gave me the time and date of the repair. It didn't happen. I called again. No change.

I pulled out the multi-page manual and found a small-print footnote, which said that the feature I desired needed a separate installation. I assumed I found the solution. I called and ordered the service.

Again, the promised due date came and went. I called again, only to learn the desired feature wasn't available in my area.

Four "customer service" people took the quick—albeit wrong—approach. They pushed me through their system and hoped it would work. Or that I'd give up. Instead, they should have taken one extra step to see if the feature was available in my area.

Had the first person taken this commonsense action, there never would have been calls two through four.

Cable Company Failure

On to cable TV. With the escalating costs of cable, it became less costly to switch to satellite. The installation and support of the satellite system was excellent. But the simple act of canceling my cable service took half a year. Each month a new bill would arrive, announcing an ever-increasing balance due.

I'd call the cable company. They'd assure me they had indeed canceled our service, and they did not know why we kept receiving bills. This continued for six months. No company can be that incompetent. I wonder if they did this on purpose to pad their receivables.

Another Telephone Company Failure

In the days of dial-up computer access (anyone remember that?), it thrilled me when my phone company offered DSL. Though the installation went as expected, the challenge came in disconnecting my old dial-up internet line. Because of a previous debacle on their part, my internet line was the billed number, and my listed number was secondary.

The representative was knowledgeable. She apologized, saying that the only solution was to cancel the entire account and then reinstall my main line. This would only be a billing function and my phone service would remain uninterrupted. But she explained that there would be side effects—many of them.

First, I would need to call their DSL division and update my billing arrangement to make sure they didn't cancel my DSL service. This must have been common because the DSL representative understood the situation and knew exactly what steps to take.

Then I would need to call my long distance carrier to ensure that when my service was "reinstalled" they would put me on my same rate plan and not their higher, default pricing tier.

Next, I had to place a third call for my white pages listing—another relic of the past.

Each call went as I hoped.

Imagine the turmoil that would have ensued had the first rep not informed me of all these ramifications and told me exactly what I needed to do. Good business practices would have never put me in the position to need to make those calls to begin with. Even adequate service would have done that work for me, but I assume the company trained the rep to tell me to make those calls, saving her the time from doing so.

Quality service didn't sell it, being the only game in town did.

Customer Service Success Tip

Turn the phrase "service sold it" from a marketing mantra into a principle that guides all your organization does.

Beware Corporate Partners

*Consider Both the Positive Potential and
Negative Consequences When Aligning with
Another Company*

Here's a long-ago story of how an affiliate lost a company a long-term customer. The experience so disillusioned me about companies working together that I still distrust any joint marketing, co-branding, or bundled services initiative. Though this is a trend in today's increasingly online business environment, it's one I avoid as a business owner and as a consumer. Here's why:

The Saga

After I graduated from high school, I applied for and received a gasoline credit card from a well-known brand that had many stations in our area. Only going to their stations, I purchased all my gas with this card.

An Affiliate Credit Card: After several years, this brand announced a partnership with a major credit card company. This would produce a branded credit card that gave discounts on gas purchases and offered other benefits. I applied for this new affiliate card and soon received their shiny piece of plastic.

Things worked well for several years.

Then a surprise came on the monthly statement, a $29 late fee. My wife called the credit card company to inquire. Since our payment history was perfect, it was a trivial matter to get the charge removed. Yet the phone rep admonished her to mail the payment earlier to avoid future late fees.

The next month, my wife mailed the payment five days before the due date. Again, another late fee appeared. This time no amount of pleading could get the charge removed.

Draconian Policies: "We don't care when you mailed your payment, nor do we consider the post-mark," came the arrogant reply. "We only use the date we post your payment."

This change in policy seemed underhanded, even more so since the credit card company applied our payment eight days after we mailed it.

"But we have no control over when you process our check," my wife countered.

The agent's response was terse. "We always post payments on the day we receive them."

We escalated our complaint, and soon the only remaining recourse was to submit our concern in writing. This produced a series of automated written responses from the credit card company. The last one promised they would notify us of their findings as soon as they became available. We received no further communication about the matter.

Lifetime Value: We stopped using this brand-ed affiliate card and began buying gasoline using a different, non-branded card. This provided flexibility since we no longer needed to buy gas from one brand. And because we didn't earn a rebate for brand purchases, we could now shop for the lowest-priced gasoline. It wasn't long before we stopped buying that brand altogether.

Over the prior twenty-four years, I estimate we spent $20,000 on that brand of gas. Our future consumption could have been another $30,000. This means the gasoline company lost a $50,000 lifetime customer and $30,000 in future business because of a $29 late fee and the unfair policies that supported it.

The Solution

What conclusions can we draw from this experience?

Scrutinize the Downside: The first is to be careful in pursuing strategic alliances. Yes, this is a business trend and, when done right, it's a smart move to keep customers and add new ones. I'm sure the gasoline brand saw these benefits, which is why they formed a relationship with the credit card company.

The failure in the company's strategy is that they relinquished financial interaction with their customers to a third party. The credit card company didn't see us as a $20,000 customer or foresee a $50,000 lifetime value. They viewed us as an unprofitable credit card holder since we always paid the entire balance each month and paid on time—or attempted to do so.

When forming any kind of marketing, cross-promotion, or reciprocal business relationship, retain control over your customers. Don't leave such a critical element to another company.

Have Fair Procedures: The second lesson is policies. Though the credit card company's decision to track late fees and interest charges by the date posted is practical and easy to apply—as well as being self-serving—is it fair? Exercise care to ensure that policies balance the needs of the company with the best interests of the customer.

Train for a Customer-First Perspective: Last, consider your staff. The agents my wife talked to did not have the latitude to credit a late fee more than once. Their supervisors didn't either, nor did the managers.

Yes, there is a place for rules, but to make them absolute handicaps staff and can ruin customer relationships. The last words that a frustrated patron wants to hear are, "It's our policy," or "I can't do that."

Because of these problems caused by a partner company, the gasoline brand, through no fault of its own, lost me as an exclusive customer and encouraged me to spend money with its competitors.

We did, however, receive a notice from the credit card company stating in part, "the gasoline company will no longer be taking part with us in a credit card program." Might the gasoline brand have realized what I've just pointed out?

Customer Service Success Tip

When pursuing strategic partnerships, affiliate initiatives, and joint ventures, temper your excitement for the positive potential with caution over the possible negative consequences.

Are there any existing initiatives you need to revisit or cancel?

The Name Game

Use Names to Facilitate Effective
Communication and Not Obscure It

In "The Perfect Answer," we talked about using your name when answering phone calls. This makes a personal connection with the caller and facilitates productive communication to result in positive outcomes.

Besides phone calls, names are equally important for online and in-person communication. Here are some further thoughts on names.

The Alias

A friend once worked for a collection agency. All day he placed calls to people who owed money to his clients. Since he was attempting to contact people who didn't want to be found, he often met with opposition and even threats. Because of this, he never used his actual name and adopted an alias for his work.

This was a company policy to protect employees from reprisals by those they pursued. Since he presented himself as a named person, he met with more success than he would've had he been a nameless voice from the dreaded collection agency.

As a side effect, assuming a new name enabled him to adopt a different persona at work. Contrary to his mellow personality, his collection agency character allowed him to become a determined sleuth unaffected by avoidance tactics and threats of retaliation.

In this case, using an alias was both safe and effective.

The Switch

While attending a banquet, it surprised me to see a friend working there as a server. Chloe shared that she took this occasional part-time work to earn extra money. After chatting a while, I glanced at her name tag. It said "Jennifer."

She smiled. "They make us wear name tags, but they never said we had to wear our own. So, we all switch." Her eyes twinkled with excitement. "Sometimes I swap with Jeremy."

Though Chloe could pass as Jennifer, she certainly didn't look like a Jeremy.

This was a fun way to add some variety to a fast-paced and demanding job. Yet her admission gave me pause. I wondered what else she and her coworkers were doing, contrary to the expectation of management. The staff's reaction to their employer's name policy hinted to workplace problems. I wondered if these issues affected their patrons in a negative way.

If your staff engages in passive-aggressive behavior, look for the underlying cause and then fix it.

The Alternate

I once had an employee with an unusual name: Johnene. When answering the phone, she always gave her name as trained. Too often, however, callers asked her to repeat it. Growing tired of this, she tried a shortened version, Johnnie. Callers now understood her name, but many repeated it with a question in their voice to confirm they heard right. She then tried John, but that made things worse. Next, she even used Joan for a bit, but it didn't feel right and confused her coworkers. She reverted to Johnene.

Sometimes names can impede communication, delaying the resolution that callers seek. It may facilitate customer service to use an alternate, more common name. But not always.

Multiple times I've called companies and had a heavily accented representative—who I suspected was halfway around the world—tell me his name was Jeff or Mike. I seriously doubted that. I realize he did this because I was unlikely to understand his actual name or be able to repeat it. Yet with such an obvious mismatch between his accent and stated name, I felt duped, distracting me from accomplishing my goal.

A better solution than to adopt a common American-sounding name might be to use a nickname or the first syllable or two of his actual name. These options would better bridge the culture implied by his accent and the goal to facilitate quick caller resolution.

The Bot

More companies are using bots for customer service. Guided by artificial intelligence, bots are computer programs that communicate with customers in a way that mimics human interaction. The goal is for people to never know they're chatting with a computer program and not an actual person.

Though I have no way of knowing how many times a bot has fooled me into thinking "Larry" was real, I know that sometimes the person I assumed I was chatting with turned out to be fake. The tipoff comes as our conversation progresses and the bot becomes less helpful. Then the bot types, "Let me get someone who can help you with that."

I recently reached out to a tech company for help. I knew the initial interaction would be computerized, but they pleased me when the chat window listed the agent's name as "Bot." This left no doubt that I was interacting with a computer program and they weren't trying to deceive me. Bot understood what I needed and routed me to the right person. We'll call this a customer service win.

Does your company use bots to trick people or help them?

Customer Service Success Tip

Consider how your employees—and apps—use names when interacting with customers. Remember that the goal is effective service. Make sure your policy on using names keeps this in mind.

~

The Myth of Self-Service

Full-Service is Not Obsolete,
Just Too Often Absent

D o you prefer self-service options or full service? Though most self-service situations
exist online, not all do. We'll start our discussion by looking at four "off-line" industries that
transitioned from full-service to self-service.

Four Historic Self-Service Examples

Self-service has existed in many industries for decades. Examples include self-serve gas pumps, grocery checkout, airline ticket sales, and banking.

1. Gas Stations: First, let's consider buying gasoline. Older drivers remember the days of full-service gas stations. In fact, people called them service
stations, because service was what they did. These

service stations had one mechanic—or more—on duty. For smaller stations, the mechanic was often the one who filled your car with gas.

You pulled into the station. An air hose lying across your path activated a bell when you drove over it. This alerted the attendant that a customer had arrived. He would scurry out to greet you.

You stayed in your car, rolled down the window, and made your request. "Fill it up, please." Often you and the attendant were on a first-name basis. As he filled your gas tank, he would wash your front windshield and sometimes the back. Next, he would offer to check your oil. (Unless he had just changed or checked it, which he remembered.)

That's not all. He would glance at your tires, and if one appeared underinflated, he would whisk a tire gauge out of his pocket to check the pressure, adding air if needed. He would also make recommendations based on other observations, such as, "Looks like you're ready for new front tires," "That muffler doesn't sound too good," or "We better look at those brakes soon."

Yes, this was a full-service operation, suggesting upsells ("Do you want to try premium today?") and cross-sell opportunities ("When do you want your oil changed?"). This wasn't a marketing strategy. It was customer service.

To save on labor or cut overhead, some stations began offering "self-service" pumps. To entice the public to pump their own fuel, the self-serve gas advertised a lower price—even though it was the same product.

Most people weren't interested in refueling their own cars, at least not until the price of gas jumped and the discount increased along with it. Still, some people swore they would never fill their own gas tanks, but over time the scarcity of full-service pumps forced them to use self-service.

Most drivers didn't want self-service, but they did so to save money, or else they had to accept it when it became the only option. Today, self-serve gas pumps are an expected way of life, but this happened because it became the only option. With self-service, it's our responsibility to keep our car in good operating condition. Now we only see a mechanic when something is wrong with our car.

2. Groceries: Then there's the grocery store. I'll admit I seldom go there. And when I do, it's only to buy a few things. I gravitate toward the self-checkout. For a few items it's faster, assuming everything works as it should. Self-checkout can also irritate by flashing commands, beeping warnings, or barking out annoying instructions. The machine gets obstinate if you do something it doesn't like.

Given the choice between standing in line for the next cashier and self-service, however, I always opt for a person. I find it far less frustrating. I can't imagine the time-consuming task of doing a large order via self-checkout. However, when the cashier lines are long, which is often the case, I'm happy to duck into the self-checkout and hope for the best. Here, self-service wins out when full-service lines grow too long. It's not that I prefer it, but it's the least objectionable option.

3. Travel: Today most people buy plane tickets online. It doesn't save time, but it gives the opportunity to check every conceivable option, finding the ideal balance between cost and convenience. I may scrutinize my options too much, but I prefer to spend an hour researching flights, times, and airports if it will save me from a long layover, an extra night in a hotel, or a couple hundred dollars on a fare.

Still, the days of calling a travel agent, giving her my travel itinerary in a few seconds, and having tickets arrive the next day provide an appealing temptation to return to full-service.

4. Banks: The banking industry is full of choices. For transactions warranting full-service, I can drive to the nearest branch or call them. For self-service, I can use an ATM, bank-by-phone, or access my account online.

The option I select depends on what I need to accomplish, but my focus is on speed and convenience. It's nice to have options: self-service for some things; full-service for others.

The Self-Service Bust

In the late 1990s, a rush of companies formed under a novel business model. They became collectively known as the dot-coms. These fledgling start-ups would forego brick-and-mortar locations to conduct business solely online. In simplistic terms, their generic business plan was that they would create a scalable website, one they could ramp up as demand for their product or service grew.

They reasoned that customer service would not be an issue. They would offer self-service options that were likewise scalable. Their business models didn't require employees to help their customers. Computers would do that over the internet. As a result, they would have no massive customer support centers to build and staff.

This self-serve idealism didn't work so well. The few companies that survived did so because they realized they needed to offer more than just self-service, expanding their support options to meet the needs of their customers. For some, this meant building the call centers they hadn't planned on or outsourcing the work to a company that specialized in customer service.

People to the Rescue

This history of self-service and its varying degrees of success doesn't imply that self-service is the solution.

This is even more true when responsive employees—either in person or at a call center—surpass the limitations of self-service.

Yes, sometimes self-service is the answer. There are also times when it isn't.

With a proper implementation of full-service, most people will opt for self-service only if it's faster, will save money, is more effective, or is more available. If it can't accomplish at least one of these tasks, people will only select self-service when they must, complaining all the while.

In truth, most consumers don't prefer self-service. What they want is full-service that is friendly, accessible, and dependable. In our global economy, that often means they want a call center—a good one.

Most shoppers don't select self-service because it is better, but because it's the least objectionable option. What's the right answer? It's a workable full-service solution from actual people.

Who would prefer to spend an hour on the internet, searching and scrolling through FAQs while waiting for an automated response to an email query, if making a phone call provided a quick and accurate response?

They're looking for a call center done right. What does this look like? The ideal is:

- Calls answered with minimum delay

- No busy signals

- First-call resolution

- No transfers

- No queue or a short queue (or a creative, entertaining on-hold program with accurate traffic queue updates)

- Trained, knowledgeable, personable, and polite representatives

- Correct responses

- Consistent experiences

Achieving this, why would anyone want self-service? Why would they ever switch to a different company because of poor service? Full-service done right will beat self-service every time.

A Place for Self-Service

But what about people who prefer self-service? Offer it.

Know that the reason people opt to do things themselves is that a lifetime of experiences has conditioned them to accept self-service as the only workable solution. Offer them a superior full-service alternative, and they'll learn to use it. You'll ingratiate them to your business.

What steps do you need to implement to provide the full-service experience that most of your customers want?

Customer Service Success Tip

Balance self-serve economy with full-service results.

A Place for Self-Service

Good Customer Service
Keeps Its Promises

Say What You'll Do and Do What You Say

Repeated stories in this book relate to cell phone companies. It's a sad commentary on the industry, yet these lessons apply to all businesses.

For cell phone companies, a disregard for existing customers and preference for new business drives existing customers to their competitors every two years. I have ample stories to share, none of them good.

What's interesting is that each switching cycle starts online and may shift to the telephone before moving to in-person to finalize the transaction. Once completed, interaction may move back to the telephone for a time before reverting to online for the long term. There is a significant disconnect between these channels.

Through the decades of the every-other-year carrier switch, I can recall none that occurred as expected. None ingratiated me to my new provider, and each one took too much time. Most incurred unexpected charges or hidden fees. *Hidden* is a generous word. *Lied to* is more common.

No carrier stands above the others in treating customers right and attempting to hold on to the ones they have rather than continually churn them.

A New Twist

Though our existing carrier was content to continue service under the terms of our original agreement, they took no steps beyond that to keep our business. It was only through the work of an independent sales unit that we learned of a plan that worked for us and would not force us to switch providers.

Key to this was a generous trade-in allowance for our existing phones. Factoring the credit into our calculations would allow us to upgrade our phones at no cost and enjoy a slight decrease in our monthly rate. It seemed too good to be true.

We scrutinized the fine print in their offer and found no flaw. The decision to upgrade service was easy. After confirming the details of their offer, we committed to move forward. Switching took much longer than it should, which happens each time we upgrade. But we walked out of the store with our new phones and began transferring information so we could use them and then return the old units.

A Shocking Development

After wiping the memory on our old phones and shipping them in to receive our trade-in rebates, we encountered a shock. They reviewed our working phones, listed made up problems, and downgraded our promised rebates to less than 10 percent of what we expected. The carrier was unwilling to discuss this. The discrepancy between their promise and their reality was a couple thousand dollars.

An online search for resolutions revealed many people who felt similarly duped. The only successful recourse was to wait three months for the final determination and then reporting them to the Better Business Bureau. Once aggrieved customers filed their complaints, the carrier made good on their promise.

That's not a wise business strategy.

Customer Service Success Tip

Uncover times your customers may have felt tricked by your marketing promotions and customer retention initiatives. Eliminate these disparities between fact and fiction.

If you don't address these issues, you'll alienate customers. And they'll tell everyone they can, further hurting your chances of gaining new business.

Put It All Together

To conclude our investigation of customer service failures and successes, we'll wrap up with some parting chapters to move you and your company forward so you can stop churning customers and start growing your business.

This applies whether the interaction occurs in person, over the telephone, or online. And it's even more important in multichannel situations where customers have options in how they contact your organization. If you fall short in one channel, they're apt to reach out to you in another. This doubles your customer service workload.

Frontline Customer Service Staff

Work to Make Your Support Staff's Job Easier

A common thread throughout this book is that a person—not a department or an organization—provides customer support. The two exceptions are self-service and automated bots, but even these often require—or, at least, should require—an actual person to back them up.

This means that your frontline employees are key to customer service success. You play a role in their work, their workload, and their associated attitude. Look for ways to make their jobs easier. Here are some actions you can take to better support them, to increase positive outcomes, and to improve their job outlook.

Review Policies

Look at your organization's procedures and rules. Do these help your customer service staff do their job better or do these items make their work harder? Balance your policies between business acumen and customer service workload. Often, well-meaning business directives subject your staff to unnecessary customer complaints and workplace frustration.

For example, one employer I worked for had an internal policy that all payments were net 45, instead of paying within the standard thirty days, which most every company expects. This caused me to spend way too much time fielding calls from frustrated vendors about delayed payments.

Empower Staff

Give your employees the authority to do the right thing for your customers. This is especially true in situations where managers have the latitude to make these decisions. Forcing customers to escalate their concerns causes more work for managers and diminishes the customer service personnel in the eyes of the caller.

Provide Supervisory Support

You can help customer service employees with wise supervision. This isn't to monitor their behavior but to assist with difficult interactions. Sometimes a customer and an employee will not mesh, no matter how hard the employee tries. Doing a handoff to a supervisor (or even a seasoned coworker) can turn an ill-fated contact into a successful one.

Fix Problems First

How much of the customer service work that your staff does results from problems your company caused? This can result from an email sent too soon, a letter mailed to the wrong customers, or a website that contains misinformation. Avoid or fix these issues to keep customers from contacting support because of your company's self-inflicted problems.

A confusing or hard-to-navigate website is another unnecessary source of customer service work. Even worse is a website that's broken. I once tried for three days to update my credit card number on a vendor's website, only to receive an error message each time. When I finally reached someone in support, she immediately understood the situation. "Sorry, but that section of our website isn't working correctly." I wonder how many needless chat sessions she, and her coworkers, endured because of this website problem.

Celebrate Their Work

Always do what you can to acknowledge the efforts of your customer service staff. Celebrate their positive outcomes and excellent work. Say, "Thank you."

This occurs directly with your words, both in person and written. Notes, emails, and memos of heartfelt appreciation go a long way to affirm the work of a too-often underacknowledged but essential part of your operation. Acknowledging their work also occurs tangibly with their paychecks and compensation packages.

I once had a boss who combined these two elements. On Fridays he would deliver our checks. He'd walk into my office, hand me my paycheck, and say "thank you." Then he'd leave to deliver the next one.

Never lose sight of the critical role you play in thanking your customer service staff for their work.

This isn't a once-and-done action, but an ongoing initiative.

Customer Service Success Tip

Make your support staff's job easier by removing roadblocks that impede them from doing their job.

How to Deal with Difficult Customers

A Personal Note to Frontline Customer Service Staff

Anyone who's worked in a support role knows how difficult it can be. Yes, some customers—hopefully most—are easy to work with and appreciative of your responses. They may even thank you for your help. Celebrate each one of these wins and use them to shape your outlook for the day.

Yet other customers, hopefully a minority, are challenging. They're agitated before they even reach you, and if you don't provide the answers they seek, their ire escalates. Even though you aren't the cause of the problem that prompted them to contact you, they dump their frustration on you anyway, sometimes erupting into a personal attack. This isn't fair. It isn't right. But it happens.

First, know that everyone who contacts you makes a choice in how they treat you. They can choose to interact with you in a respectful and humane way. Or they can choose to let their emotions control the words they say and how they speak to you. This is on them, not you. This explanation doesn't excuse their behavior, but it helps us better understand it.

Next, your responses to these difficult customers can defuse the situation or worsen it. Just as their decision of how to treat you is within their control, your reaction to them is within yours.

Here are some tips to defuse difficult customer service situations.

Remain Calm

It's hard to maintain your composure amid confrontation. Yet this is key to successfully dealing with challenging people. Don't mirror their unruly behavior and reflect their negativity. Instead, counter their inappropriate conduct with an appropriate response.

If your interaction is over the phone, don't forget to breathe. This will help you relax. It also releases tension. Remember to smile. A smile on your face will ease helpful words out of your mouth. Some reps place a small mirror on their desk to remind them to smile. Callers will hear your smile. Also be professional, treating them as you would want them to treat you.

Though not as critical when you're not on the phone, these tips to breathe, smile, and be professional also apply to online interactions, such as text chat, email, and social media.

Pause

If you feel emotion building up inside of you that might cause you to say something that's not helpful, pause. If you're on the phone, you can ask them to hold while you "look something up." The same applies to chat. You can also introduce a pause into email and social media support without the customer even knowing it.

When receiving an emotion-filled email, I make myself wait an hour before responding, sometimes even waiting until the next day. My delayed communication is always more constructive than what I would have typed at first.

Regardless of how you pause a customer interaction, the purpose is for you to refocus your attention on producing a positive outcome and to ensure you don't respond negatively and escalate the situation.

End Positively

Regardless of the customer service outcome, make sure you conclude it positively. You can thank the customer for contacting you—even if you don't want to say so. Or end by telling them to enjoy the rest of their day.

This accomplishes two things.

For the customer, it may cause them to rethink what just happened, hopefully putting their day on a different trajectory.

For you, it helps set the tone for your next customer interaction. It signals to your mind and body that the difficult interaction is over, and it's time to embrace the next one with a fresh outlook.

Take a Break

Sometimes after you complete a negative customer service interaction, you need time to move past it. This makes sure you don't carry the unpleasant situation you just endured into your next call.

You may need to take a break.

Most employers understand this and allow their customer service reps the latitude to take this step as needed. This action, however, should be rare and not the norm. If your employer doesn't allow this, then do what you can to interject a short pause into your workflow after a difficult call.

Customer Service Success Tip

Work to make every customer interaction produce a positive outcome. Celebrate your successes. Learn how to better deal with difficult customers. Don't let one rude customer ruin your day.

Working in customer service has many rewarding moments. Don't lose sight of them.

Move Forward

Every business and nonprofit has a customer service element. Sometimes customer service exists as a department, and in other instances it's part of a person's duties or job description. At times, service lurks behind the scenes. Stakeholders expect it, and providers deliver it, without either party recognizing that customer service occurred. Yet it did.

I hope you gleaned helpful insights from these stories. Sometimes we upheld excellences to strive for, yet too many times we detailed failures to avoid.

Will you apply the tips in this book to your work? Or will you set these words aside, soon forget them, and return to business as usual?

The choice is yours.

The wise response is to pick one customer service success tip, focus on it, and enact improvements. Then move to the next item and pursue it. Move through all twenty-eight tips. When you finish, start over to embark on another round of incremental customer service improvements.

Customer service isn't a once-and-done effort. It's not a set-it-and-forget-it initiative. It takes an ongoing effort to truly meet your customers' expectations.

I hope this book points you in that direction.

* * *

To receive an email when the next Sticky book comes out, sign up at PeterLyleDeHaan.com.

Books by
Peter Lyle DeHaan

For a complete, up-to-date list of Peter's books, go to PeterLyleDeHaan.com.

Sticky Series Books

- Sticky Leadership: Lead Well to Produce Business Success and Inspire Employees

- Sticky Sales and Marketing: Market with Honor and Sell with Integrity to Produce Sustainable Outcomes

- Sticky Living: Live a Life that Matters to Your Family, Friends, and Community

Other Books

- The Successful Author

- How to Start a Telephone Answering Service

About Peter Lyle DeHaan

Peter Lyle DeHaan, PhD, is an entrepreneur and business owner who has managed, owned, and started multiple businesses over his career. Common themes at every turn have included customer service, sales and marketing, and leadership and management. He shares his lifetime of business experience and personal insights with others through his books, articles, and blogs to encourage, inspire, and occasionally entertain.

Learn more at PeterLyleDeHaan.com.

www.ingramcontent.com/pod-product-compliance
Lightning Source LLC
Chambersburg PA
CBHW071212210326
41597CB00016B/1777